AF584312

The marvellous manner of water.

PHILIP BUNTING

Have you ever noticed that you're a little bit squishy? That's because more than half of your body is water! All life on Earth – from blue whales to bacteria, yew trees to you – depends upon water. Water flows through us all, and we wouldn't be here without it.

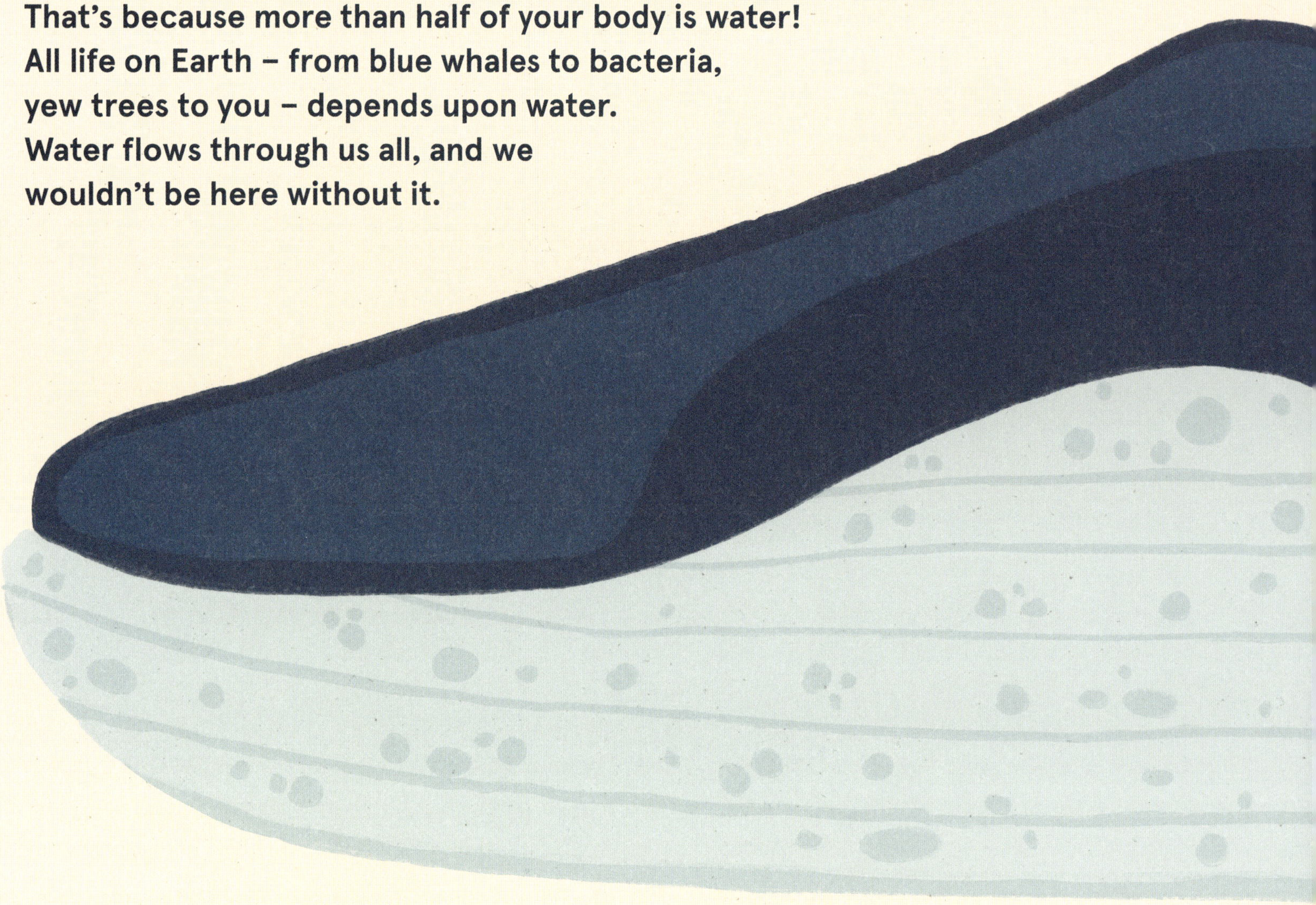

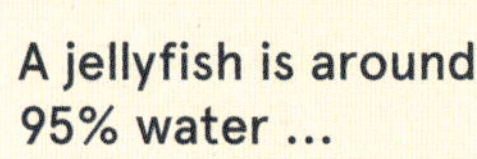

A jellyfish is around 95% water ...

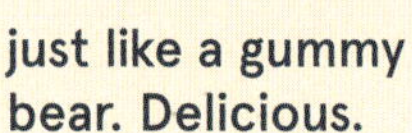

just like a gummy bear. Delicious.

A potato is roughly 80% water.

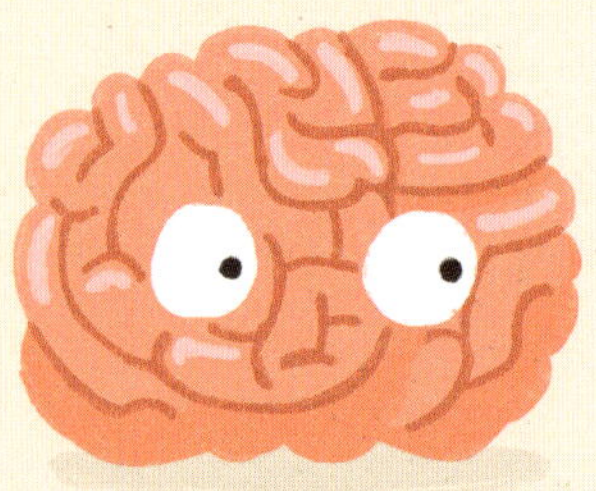

Your brain is around 75% water ...

that's very similar to this banana (was 75%).

Trees are around 75% water too.

Bacteria contain around 70% water.

We are 60% water. Or thereabouts.

About 3% of Antarctic ice is penguin pee.

This book contains up to 10% water!

Upon first inspection, water can seem a little so-so, ho-hum and even hum-drum.

It is colourless, tasteless, can't tell jokes, and doesn't even have a smell ...

yet water can be lots of fun!

Water seems soft and gentle, however
it has the force to shape our world.
But what is water?

Let's start small. Really small.
All bodies of water – from a cloud, to an ocean, to a snowflake – are made of many tiny parts, called molecules.

A water molecule is made of three even tinier parts: two hydrogen atoms and one oxygen atom.

There would be around

1,500,000,
000,000,000,
000,000,000,
000

(1.5 sextillion!) water molecules in a drop this size:

H_2Woah.

Thanks to its many marvellous molecules, water can exist in one of three states:

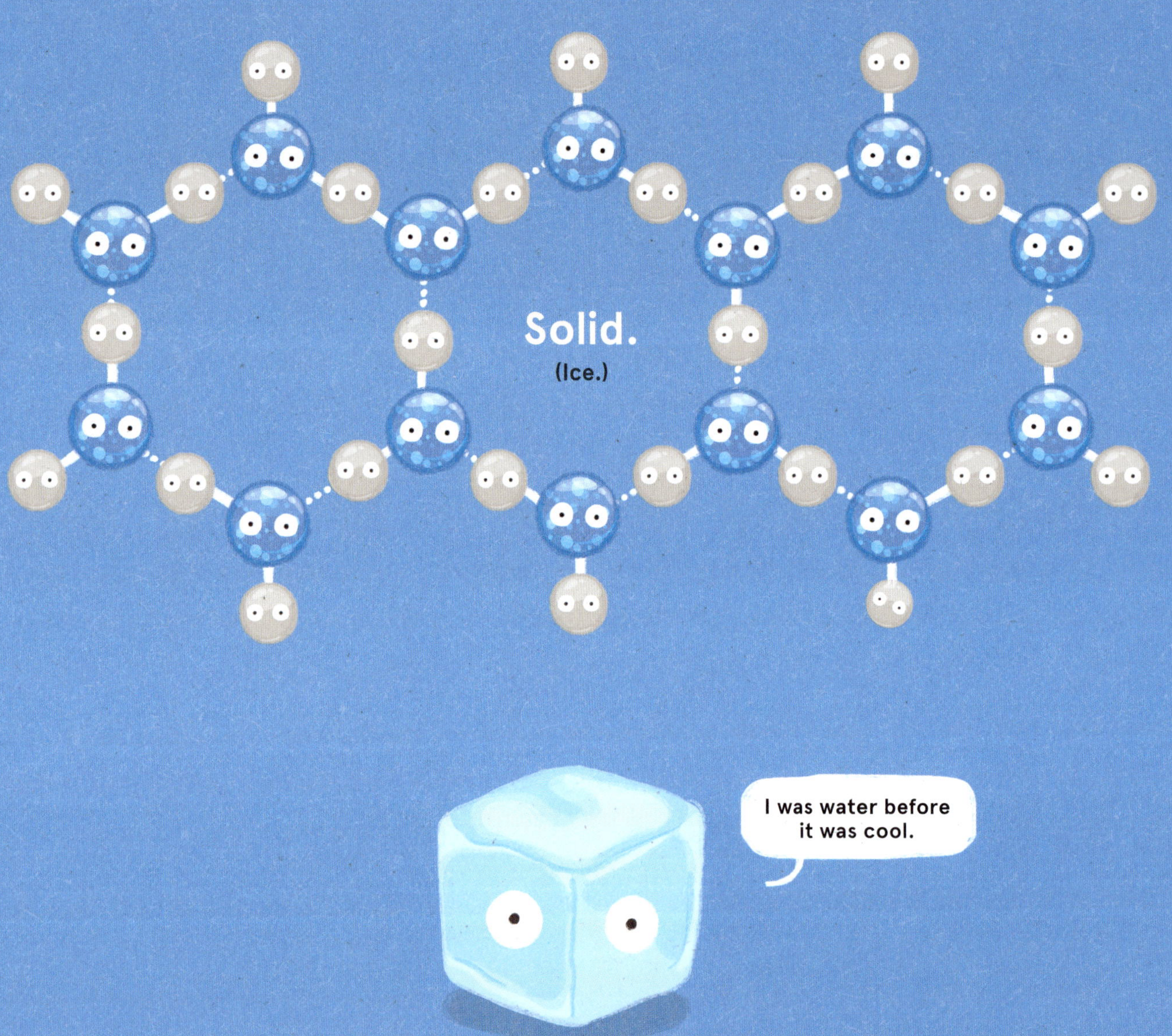

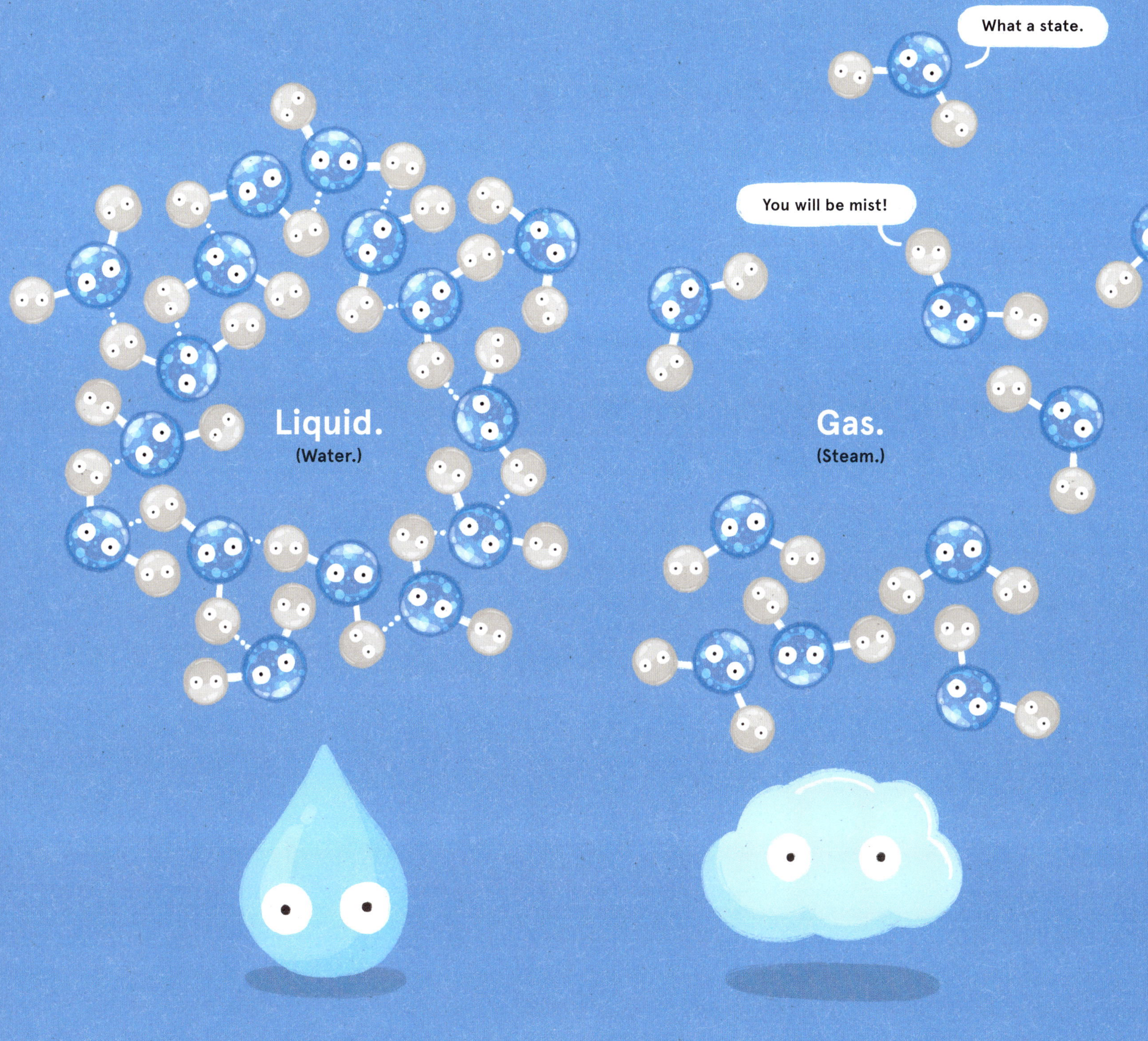

Depending on the conditions of its environment, water adapts to suit the world around it, flowing to the most suitable state without a thought.

Here on Earth, liquid water is pretty much everywhere. Luckily for us, our home planet sits in a Goldilocks zone, where the conditions are not too hot and not too cold (they're just right) for water to exist as a liquid.

Mercury.
No liquid water here. Mercury is way too close to the sun.

Venus.
No liquid water here either (still too hot at a toasty 475°C).

Earth.
Water covers around 71% of our beautiful blue planet's surface.

Mars.
Has frozen water at its poles, and possibly in underground lakes!

Jupiter.
No water here! This gassy giant is mostly hydrogen and helium.

Saturn.
No water here either, however many of Saturn's 82 moons are made mostly of frozen water.

Uranus.
The stinkiest planet is made of frozen water, methane and ammonia.

Neptune.
This frozen giant has heaps of ice, but no liquid water.

But how did we end up with so much water here on Earth?

Most water molecules arrived when our planet formed. They happened to be in the dust cloud that went on to become our solar system.

Achoo!

Later, other water molecules made it to Earth by hitching a ride on frozen comets.

But once they had landed here on Earth, there was no escape. The same water molecules have been cycling around our world for billions of years.

So while that glass of water might appear a little so-so, ho-hum or even hum-drum at first glance, it didn't simply spring from your local lake ...

the water in your glass was formed billions of years ago ... in Space!

This spectacular space juice helps control the temperature of Earth. Flowing currents in the ocean move warm water away from the equator, keeping temperatures just right for life to thrive all around our precious planet.

At any given time, around 97% of the water on Earth is salty and therefore undrinkable!

The fresh water we all rely upon is made possible thanks to a phenomenon known as the water cycle ...

Whether quickly rising through the atmosphere or slowly bobbing down a river, water molecules constantly flow from one state or place to the next. Water is always in motion, always on its way to becoming something else.

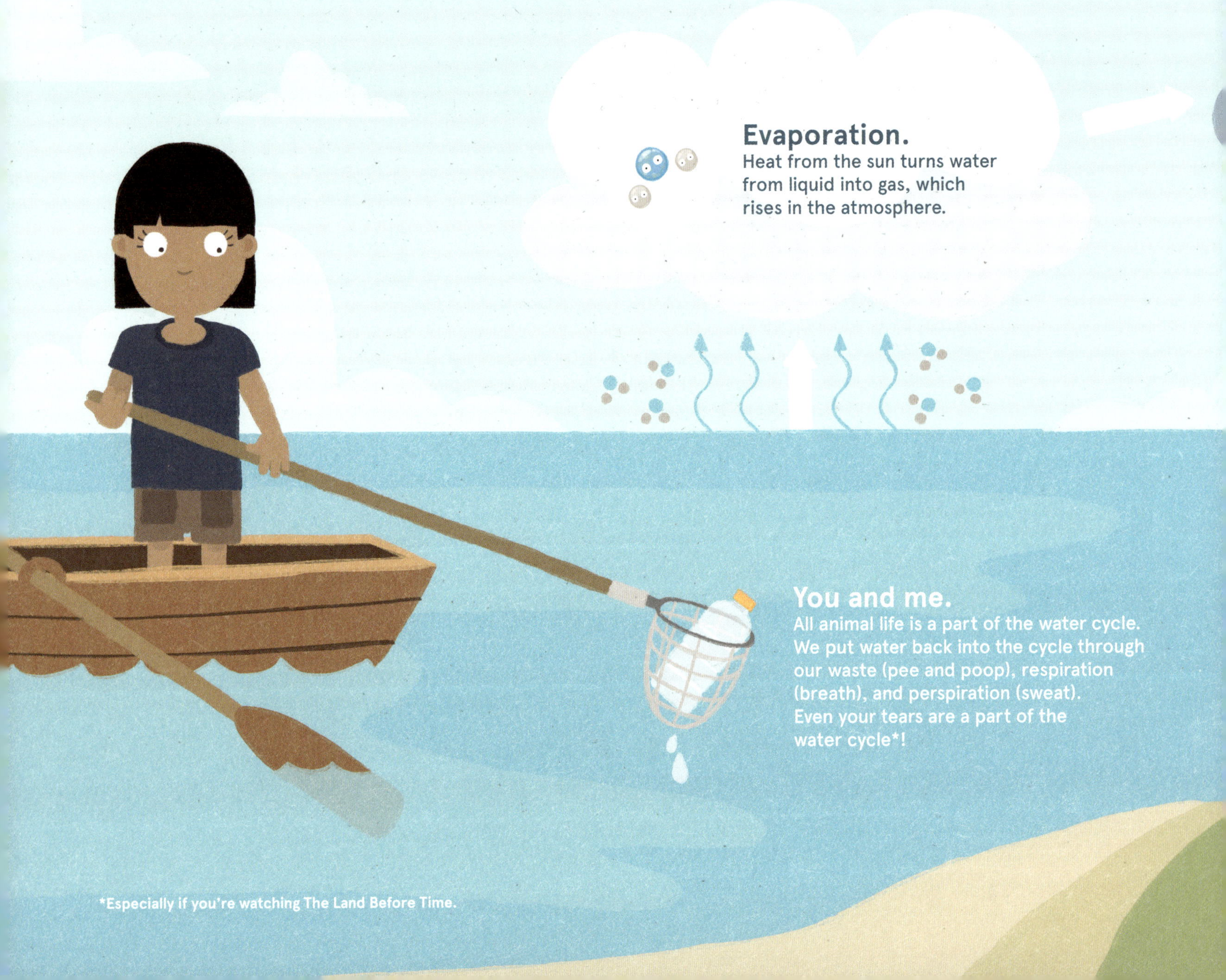

Evaporation.

Heat from the sun turns water from liquid into gas, which rises in the atmosphere.

You and me.

All animal life is a part of the water cycle. We put water back into the cycle through our waste (pee and poop), respiration (breath), and perspiration (sweat). Even your tears are a part of the water cycle*!

*Especially if you're watching The Land Before Time.

Precipitation.
Once enough liquid water has gathered and cooled, it falls back to the earth as rain, hail or snow.
Condensation.
The higher it gets, the cooler it gets. The gas eventually cools and condenses into liquid water.
Transpiration.
During photosynthesis, some water evaporates from the surface of plants' leaves, becoming water vapour.
The 'C'.

Those same old water molecules have been flowing in the same old cycle for billions of years. It is highly likely that pretty much every water molecule in your glass once, err, passed through a dinosaur and countless other lifeforms before them!

Don’t drink that.

All life (including you) is a part of the water cycle. For as long as life flows through you, so does water.

The persistent movement of water forms the world around us. Streams, rivers, valleys, lakes, and even entire continents are shaped by the patient, consistent action of water.

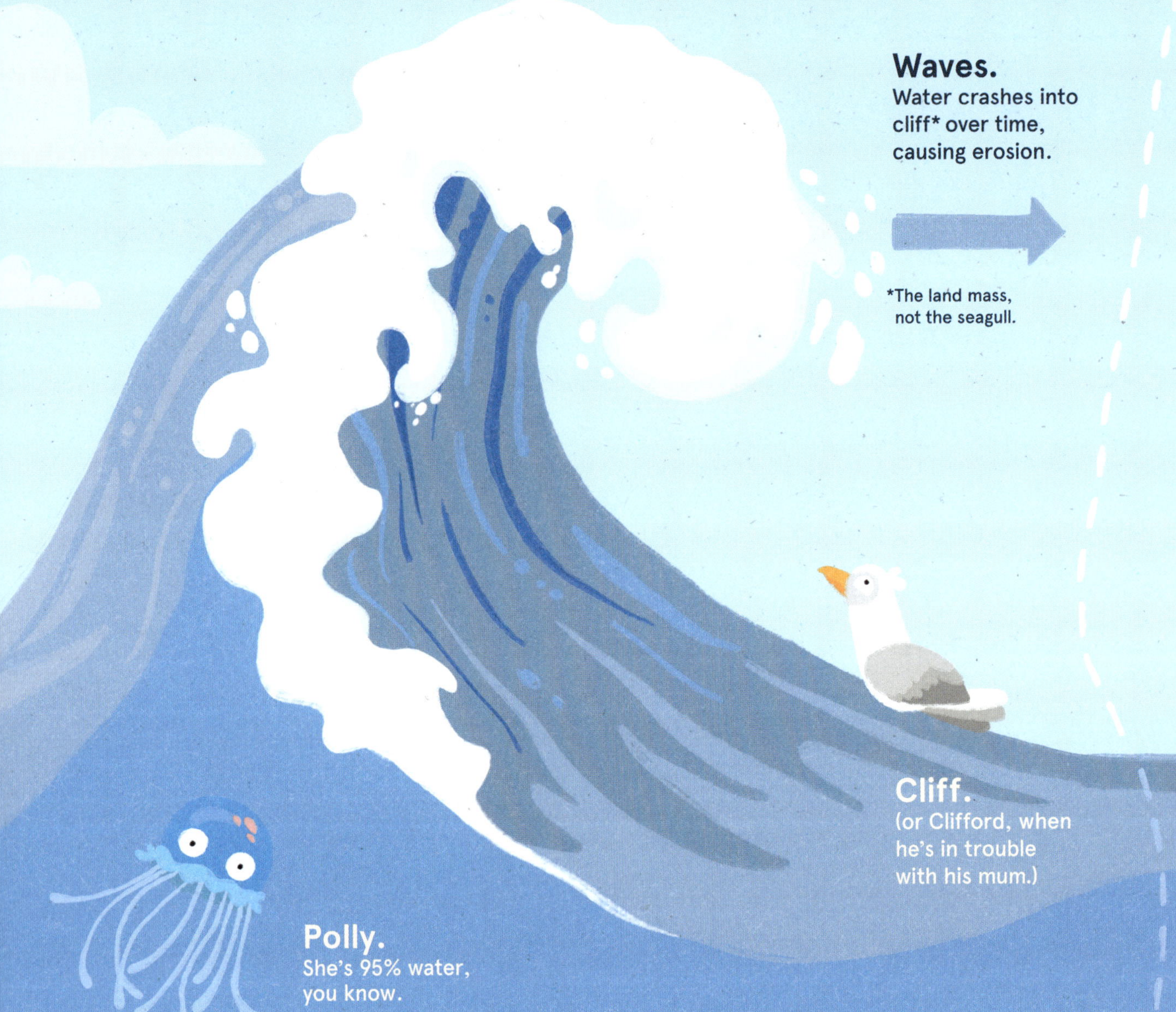

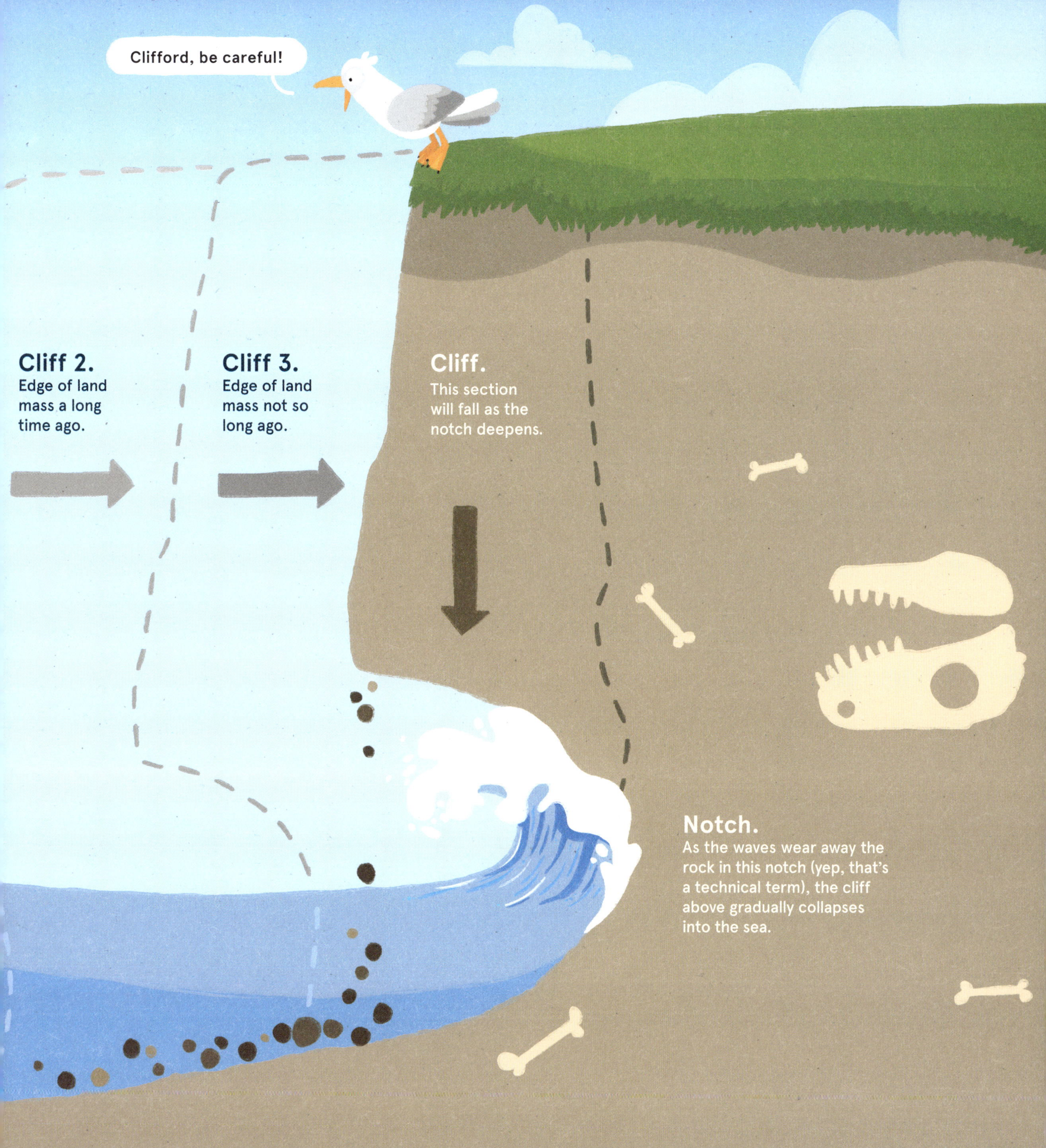
Clifford, be careful!
Cliff 2.
Edge of land mass a long time ago.
Cliff 3.
Edge of land mass not so long ago.
Cliff.
This section will fall as the notch deepens.
Notch.
As the waves wear away the rock in this notch (yep, that's a technical term), the cliff above gradually collapses into the sea.

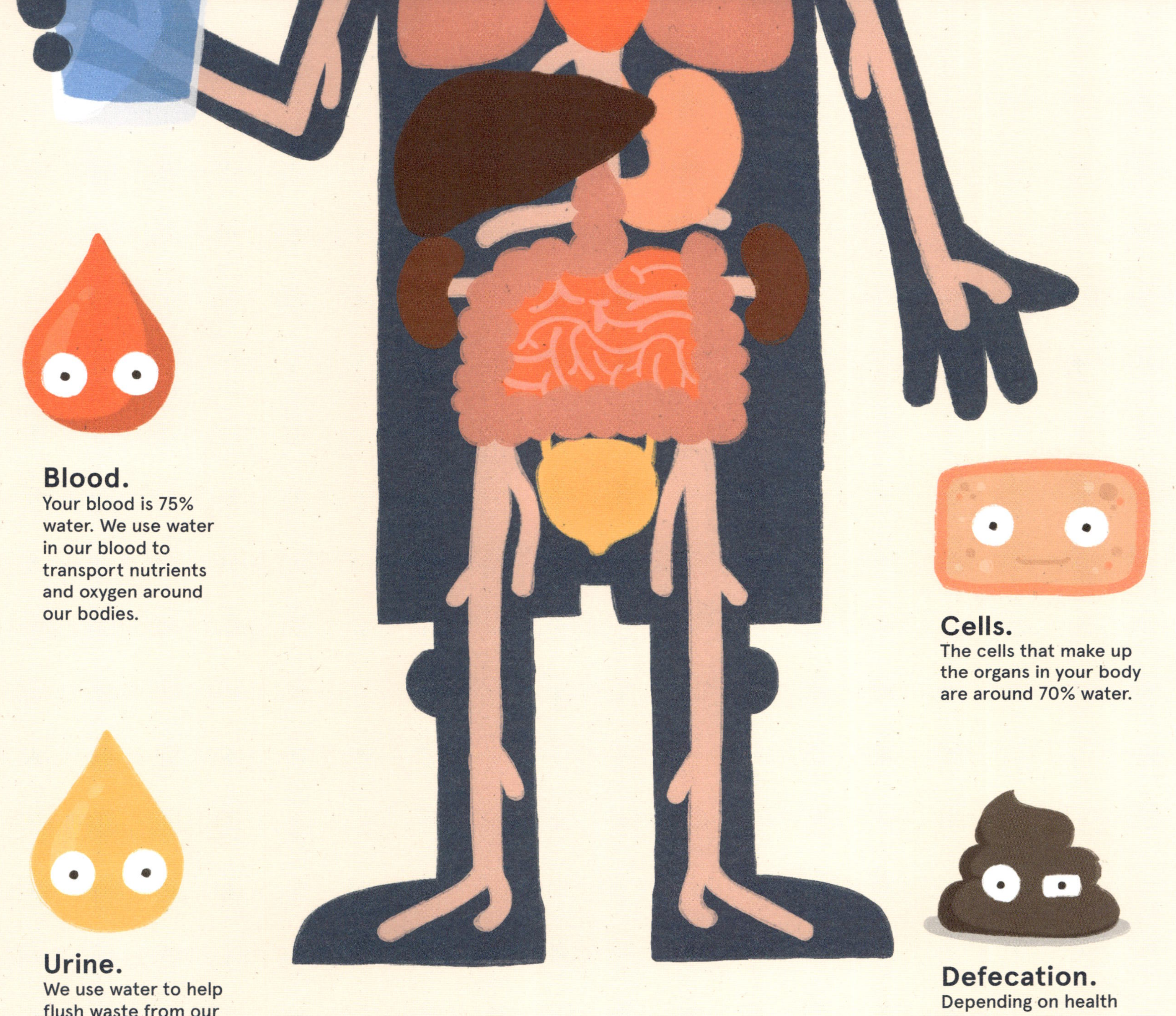

Blood.
Your blood is 75% water. We use water in our blood to transport nutrients and oxygen around our bodies.

Urine.
We use water to help flush waste from our bodies. Your pee contains around 95% water.

Cells.
The cells that make up the organs in your body are around 70% water.

Defecation.
Depending on health and diet, our poop contains around 75% water.

As we go about our business, we hairy humans each lose litres of water per day through our pee, poop, sweat, and breath (and tears, if we graze a knee). We replace that lost water through food and drink, so that our brilliant bodies can continue to do their thing:

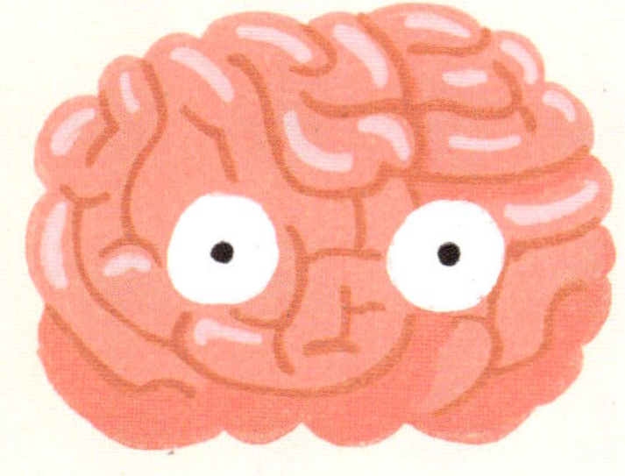

Brain.
Water carries essential oxygen and nutrients to your busy brain, as well as creating a protective layer around it.

Respiration.
We each exhale around a cup of water each day through our breath!

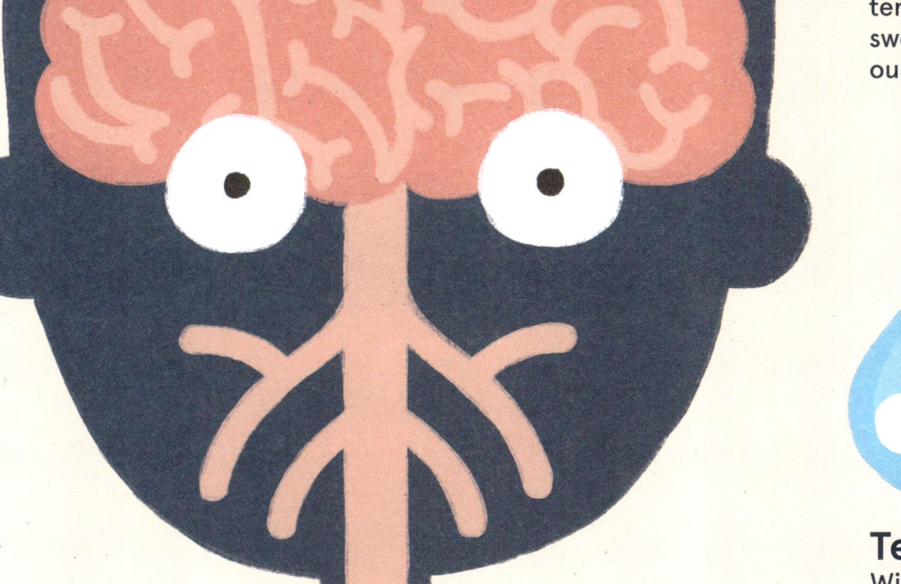

Perspiration.
We use water to help regulate our body temperature, by sweating through our skin.

Tears.
Without even blinking an eyelid, our bodies use water to create tears, to keep our vision clear.

Because it works with natural forces, liquid water will always flow to the lowest point it can find. In doing so, water helps the smallest and lowliest things to grow. In turn, these little things help the bigger things to survive and thrive.

Water is all around us: above, below and within us all.
None of us would be here without it. From one perspective,
we *are* water (even more so if you had soup for lunch).
And sometimes, it can help to be like water ...

Water reminds us that everything changes, everything flows, all the time. With an open mind, we can adapt to make the most of our time on Earth.

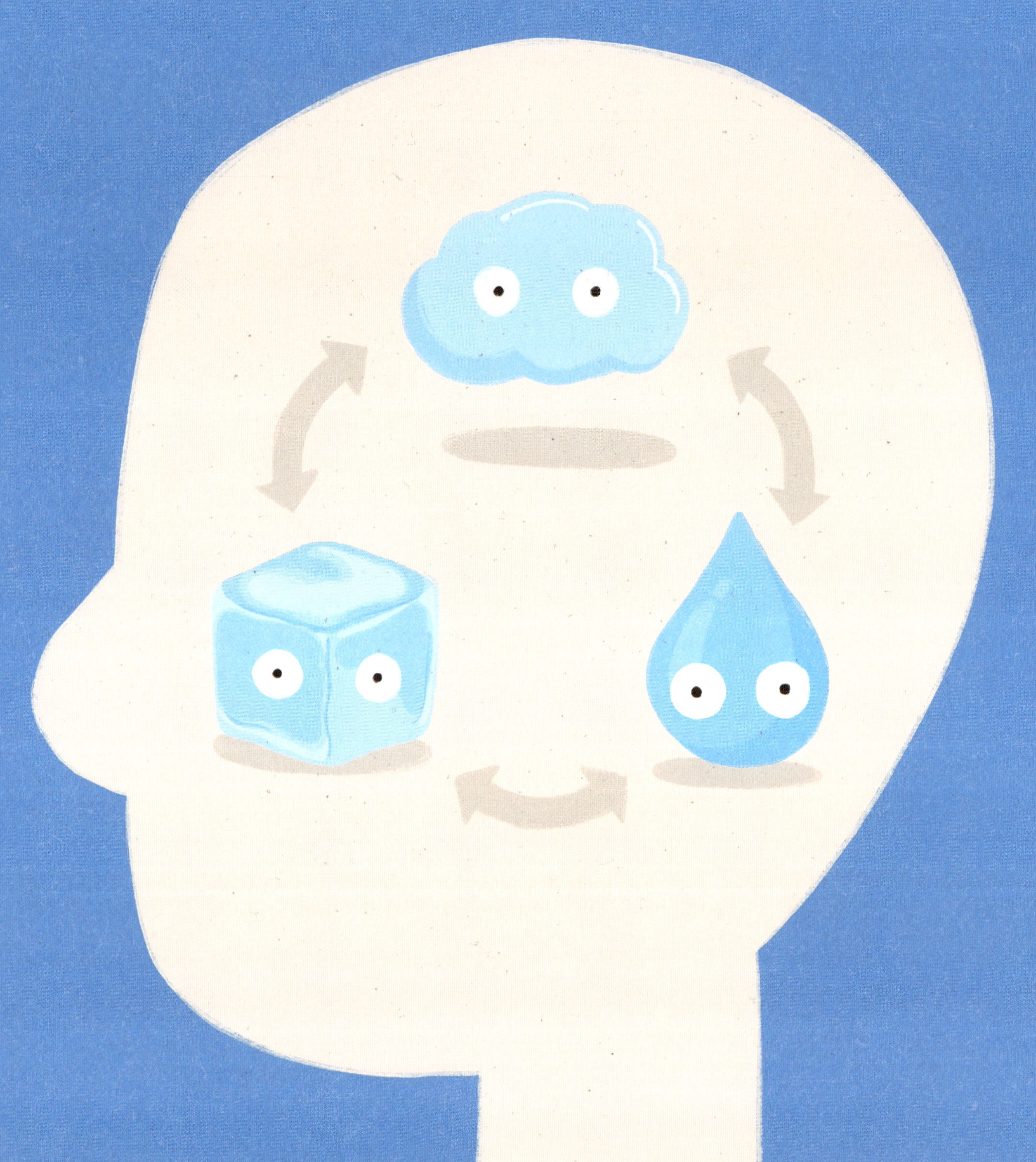

Through gentle, persistent action over time, we can help shape our little corner of the world.

Like water, we should do our best to stay humble and help those around us to live and grow (especially the little ones).

All life on Earth is connected through water. It reminds us that we are a part of something much greater, older and marvellous.

Wherever this world takes you, it might just help to be like water, and ...

go with the flow.

"Everything flows."

Heracliitus.

Omnibus Books
an imprint of Scholastic Australia Pty Ltd
(ABN 11 000 614 577)
PO Box 579, Gosford NSW 2250.
www.scholastic.com.au

Part of the Scholastic Group
Sydney • Auckland • New York • Toronto • London • Mexico City •
New Delhi • Hong Kong • Buenos Aires • Puerto Rico

First published in 2022.

A catalogue record for this book is available from the National Library of Australia

ISBN: 978-1-76097-518-0

Printed in China by RR Donnelley. Scholastic Australia's policy, in association with RR Donnelley, is to use papers that are renewable and made efficiently from wood grown in responsibly managed forests, so as to minimise its environmental footprint.
10 9 8 7 6 5 4 3 24 25 26 / 2

I acknowledge the traditional custodians of the land on which I live and work, and I pay respect to the Gubbi Gubbi nation.
I pay respects to the Elders of the community and extend my recognition to their descendants. Philip Bunting